T0060665

All About
Stephen Hawking

All About
Stephen Hawking

Chris Edwards

Indianapolis, Indiana

All About Stephen Hawking, 2nd edition

Copyright © 2017, 2021 by Chris Edwards

Published by Blue River Press
Indianapolis, Indiana
www.brpressbooks.com

Distributed by Cardinal Publishers Group
A Tom Doherty Company, Inc.
www.cardinalpub.com

First Edition: 978-1-68157-094-5
Second Edition: 978-1-68157-208-6
Ebook ISBN: 978-1-68157-212-3
LCCN: 2019957255

Author: Chris Edwards
Editor: Dani McCormick
Interior Illustrator: Amber Calderon
Book Design: Dave Reed
Cover Artist: Jennifer Mujezinovic
Cover Design: David Miles

Printed in the United States of America

26 25 24 23 22 21   2 3 4 5 6 7

Contents

Preface

Stephen Hawking was one of the great geniuses of scientific history. He strove to make the world recognize him for what he could do rather than for what he could not do.

Stephen Hawking spent much of his life trying to figure out what happens at the edge of black holes. He asked questions about what happens when light falls into a black hole. He even wondered what would happen if a person fell into a black hole!

Dr. Hawking believed that science should be understood by everyone, so he made his work understandable to everyone, not just scientists. He wrote best-selling books, appeared on many television shows, and was the subject of several biographies and movies. He was a celebrity and a scientist. He could only move a few muscles in his face, but was known for his sense of humor and personality. His body might have been stuck in a wheelchair, but Dr. Hawking's mind explored the universe.

Hawking was a scientist first and a celebrity second, but he used his fame to help people. He frequently talked about the need for wheelchair access to buildings. Stephen was a "guest" on *The Simpsons* television show and *Star Trek: The Next Generation*. Two movies have been made about his life, and one of the actors that played Stephen won an Oscar.

Stephen won major awards for his work in science and for advocating for disabled people. He was a genius and an inspiration. He was also a father of three, a grandfather to three, and a friend to many.

Chapter 1
Growing Up

On September 1, 1939, Germany invaded Poland, starting World War II. After the German army, led by Adolf Hitler, took over Poland, it conquered several other countries, including France, in a short period of time.

The British resolved not to give up and fought back against Hitler and his armies. The German Air Force flew high in the skies over London and other British cities to drop bombs on the buildings below.

The war was still raging when Stephen Hawking was born on January 8, 1942 in Oxford, England. For some reason, Germany decided not to bomb Oxford. There are multiple theories as to why this was. Many argue that Hitler wanted to use Oxford as his capital if he invaded Britain, others claim that he respected the university at the center of the town enough to leave it alone.

This famous school was named after the town and called Oxford University. Stephen's parents, who had been students at Oxford University, fled there during the war because of the university's relative safety.

Isobel Hawking always encouraged her children to read and learn about anything they were interested in.

Stephen's mother was Isobel Walker. She had six brothers and sisters, but her parents believed so strongly in education that they found a way to send Isobel to college at Oxford University. Women had only been able to officially graduate from Oxford University since 1920, but had been attending for much longer. Isobel was a student in the 1930's, but was still looked down upon for being a woman. She took classes in a variety of subjects and got degrees in economics, politics, and philosophy.

Frank Hawking studied diseases
and how they affected populations.

Frank Hawking, Stephen's father, was older than Isobel and had graduated from Oxford University before she began attending. He was interested in medicine and was in Eastern Africa studying diseases when Germany invaded Poland. He left Africa to join the British army, and because he was so well-educated, the army put him in medical research.

Even though Isobel had graduated from Oxford University, she was rejected from jobs she was qualified for due to her gender. She became frustrated and ended up as a medical secretary. She met Frank Hawking, a young researcher, while working at the National Institute for Medical Research. They quickly got married. Frank went on to earn a degree in medicine and became an epidemiologist, a person who studies diseases.

Frank and Isobel did not live in Oxford, but moved there because of Germany's frequent bombings. They thought that staying there would be safer than London, where their house was located. They stayed in a hotel until shortly after Isobel gave birth to Stephen.

World War II ended in 1945 around the time that Stephen became a big brother. His little sister Mary was born in 1943, and Phillippa was born

Stephen was born in Oxford during World War II
on the 300th anniversary of Galileo's death.

in 1947. The Hawkings lived in a suburb north of London called High Gate. Much of London and the areas around it had been damaged or destroyed by the bombs the German airplanes had dropped. Anyone who lived in a house that was still standing could expect a lot of visits from people in their family.

The Hawkings let a lot of friends and family stay at their house, which was one of the few still

Stephen had two sisters, Philippa (left) and Mary (right), that he enjoyed playing with.

standing. The Hawking family also had a beehive in the basement, so Stephen grew up with bees instead of cats or dogs.

All of the people visiting and the beehive in the basement made for a pretty strange childhood. Yet young Stephen was just like the other neighborhood boys. He played with friends in the large craters that the German bombs left near where he lived. He liked toy trains and board games, but didn't spend much time kicking soccer balls or learning to box like some boys his age.

In 1950, when Stephen was eight, his father took a new job, and the Hawkings moved to a town farther north and outside of London called St. Albans. The new Hawking house was full of books, and the children read all of the time, which suited Stephen. Sometimes, dinners would be spent in complete silence, with everyone reading a book. In addition to reading, Frank, Isobel, and Stephen liked to listen to opera on the radio.

During Stephen's childhood, the Hawkings vacationed in an old gypsy caravan at the beach.

That summer, the Hawking family took a vacation in a large wooden caravan that had once been used by traveling gypsies. The Hawking family went to the English coast and camped in the caravan. The Hawking children slept inside while the parents slept in a nearby tent. Other people in the area thought the caravan looked bad and tried to force the Hawking family to leave. But Frank Hawking said his family was not going anywhere and told everyone to just get used to the van.

Stephen attended St. Albans High School for Girls when he was in elementary school.

Shortly after returning from their vacation, Stephen was sent to the St. Albans High School for Girls, a local Christian school. It was not just a high school, it was not just for girls, and it did not only accept Christians. Elementary kids, boys, and non-Christians also attended. Stephen was not at the school for very long, though. His dad went to study diseases in Africa again, so Stephen's mom took the rest of the family to visit friends in Spain.

When the Hawking family returned to England, Stephen scored well enough on his exams to be admitted to St. Albans School. It was a well-respected middle school. When Stephen attended, the school was already over 1,000 years old.

Stephen impressed his teachers with his intelligence, even though his grades were near the bottom of the class. He did not always like to do his homework. Stephen was also not very healthy and spent a lot of time sick in bed, not in class.

Stephen Hawking did nothing as a ten or eleven-year old boy that would make people think he was a genius. He did a good job on his tests and made it into the advanced classes, but he also played games and hung out with his friends. Stephen and his friends talked about science once in a while, but not very often.

Hawking loved to play board games and would challenge his friends to a game of chess.

As Stephen got a little older, his mom would take him and his sisters to a science museum. While she stayed with his sisters, Stephen would wander the halls and look at anything that interested him. Stephen enjoyed the museum and liked learning about science in a way he wasn't taught at school.

Stephen Hawking's dad hoped that his son would become a doctor like him, but young Stephen could never see himself as a doctor. He wasn't sure what he wanted to do, but he couldn't get excited about medicine. Stephen's father tried to interest his son in diseases and viruses. Instead Stephen's math teacher, Dikran Tahta, got him interested in numbers. Tahta so deeply affected Stephen that he would work in numbers for the rest of his life. Stephen found that he liked figuring out math problems. He began to think that he could do math at the most difficult levels if he tried.

Dikran Tahta, Stephen's teacher, showed him how interesting math could be.

At the age of twelve, Stephen Hawking liked playing games, running outside, talking with his friends, and being with his mom, dad, and sisters. He was just a normal kid. As a teenager, Stephen began being interested in physics and the stars.

He heard about a new theory that said the universe was getting bigger. Stephen began to think about the universe expanding. This really changed the way he thought of the world. At thar time, it was thought that the universe was stable and unchanging. An expanding universe meant that everything was moving and changing all the time!

When Stephen turned fourteen, Frank and Isobel adopted a baby boy named Edward. Stephen was too old to enjoy playing children's games with Edward; he liked more complicated games like chess. Stephen had problems relating to his little brother, and the two did not develop much of a relationship. His sisters were closer to Edward's age and got along better with him. Stephen liked his adopted brother, but they didn't share interests. Even when he got older, Edward was never interested in books or science, and the two never had much to talk about.

Chapter 2
Off to Oxford

Hawking graduated high school early and was
eager to start learning about the universe.

Ever since he was young, Stephen liked to tear
things apart to see how they worked. As he got
to the end of high school, he became interested
in building new machines. Stephen and some
of his friends, helped by Dikran Tahta, cobbled
together a computer from spare parts. They

named it the Logical Uniselector Computing Engine and called it LUCE (Lucy). Stephen enjoyed putting the computer together more than studying.

His grades were in the middle of his class, but Stephen wanted to go to Oxford University like his mom and dad. Oxford was a very good school and hard to get into, even with good grades.

The other students preparing to go to the university were a year older than Stephen, who was just seventeen. People advised Stephen to wait a year, but Stephen really wanted to go. For the first time, he studied really hard.

Stephen was one of only three boys to enter the physics department, so most of his classes were with older boys.

When Stephen took his test, he got an almost perfect score on the physics part of his entrance exam. He impressed one of the professors at his entrance interview with his humor and charming personality. In the end, his test score and interview won the school over, and he was admitted. In 1959, Stephen Hawking was only seventeen years old and attending Oxford University on a scholarship.

When college started in the fall, Stephen felt out of place. Many of the other students in his class had just gotten out of the military and were older than him. Stephen was still a teenager and one of only three other young men to join the physics department during the fall semester.

Before he started at Oxford, the Hawkings took family photos, including a photo of Stephen and Isobel.

The first year, Stephen read science fiction books and grew out his hair. He listened to a lot of music and skipped class. He found the classes to be too easy, and he often got bored. He was only required to take one test at the end of his third year, so he didn't see why he needed to go every day.

Stephen was young and shy. He did not make many friends during his first year and a half at Oxford. He decided he needed to be more social, so he tried out for the rowing team.

Stephen had never played sports, so his back was not very strong and he could not row a boat quickly through the water. Instead, Hawking

After joining the rowing team, Stephen earned a daredevil reputation for guiding his boats through rocky waters.

became a coxswain, which meant he sat at the front of the boat and yelled instructions at the young men rowing. Acting as a coxswain was as close to being an athlete as Stephen Hawking ever got.

Hawking himself said that he did not work very hard as a student while at Oxford. Many of the other people in his class did not either, or at least it looked that way. In order to fit in, most students acted like they did not care about school work. The cool thing to do was to act as if going to class did not matter.

Stephen always loved a good joke and enjoyed taking silly pictures with his friends.

Even if he acted as if he did not to care about his class work, Stephen graduated with an honors diploma.

During his exit exam, he was supposed to show what he had learned. However, Stephen hadn't studied very much. He decided to only answer the theoretical physics questions and left all of the factual questions blank. With his degree on the line, he was called in for a final interview to decide whether he would graduate or not.

The interviewers asked him why they should let him graduate. He replied simply that if they passed him, he would continue for an advanced degree at Cambridge. It they didn't, he would return to Oxford. He ended up being allowed to graduate and went on for his doctorate at Cambridge University.

After a trip to the Middle East during his summer break, Stephen Hawking became a student at Cambridge University in the fall of 1962.

Stephen graduated from Oxford in 1962, joining a list of alumni that includes 28 British Prime Ministers, 55 Nobel Prize winners, and 120 Olympic medal winners

All of the astronomy students, including Stephen, wanted Dr. Fred Hoyle as their professor. He was the most famous and well-respected astronomer at the time. He had coined the term "The Big Bang," but did not agree with the theory that the universe was expanding. Instead, he argued that the universe was constant and had not changed.

Hoyle was already too busy with his work and other students to be Stephen's professor.

Instead, Stephen was assigned to Dennis Sciama. At first, Stephen was disappointed, but Sciama was to cosmology what Hoyle was to astronomy. Sciama later became known as one of the founders of modern cosmology. He helped Stephen form many of his famous theories.

While at Cambridge, Hawking began to think that something was not quite right with the theory of the universe that most scientists, including Dr. Hoyle, believed at the time. According to them, all of the planets, stars, and comets of the universe did not move very much in relation to other planets, stars, and comets.

This meant that the universe did not begin or end, but had always been there. This didn't make sense to Hawking. Instead, he thought that the universe expanded outward, like a balloon being blown up. This alternative theory had been named "The Big Bang" by Dr. Hoyle and had been growing in support for years.

When Stephen started attending classes, he noticed his health was getting worse. He had always gotten sick easily, but now he felt bad most of the time. He was only twenty years old and didn't know what was wrong with him.

Chapter 3
Stephen and Jane

Cambridge University was established in 1209, making it the fifth oldest university in the world.

At the beginning of the fall semester, Stephen moved into a new dorm at Cambridge. To get to know his neighbors, he went to a party. Jane Wilde, a friend of his sister, caught his attention and the two began to talk. Stephen found Jane fascinating and learned that they had a lot in common.

Jane had grown up in St. Albans near Stephen. Her parents were Christian missionaries, and Jane shared their faith. Jane and Stephen had actually gone to elementary school together in St. Albans. She was a couple years younger than Stephen, so they probably had never met in elementary school. When they met at the party, Jane had just finished high school and was about to attend the University of London. Jane wanted to earn an advanced degree on medieval literature.

Stephen was normally shy around girls, but he thought Jane was so pretty and intelligent that he made an effort to continue talking with her. Jane thought Stephen was cute and funny. Before the party was over, Stephen got Jane's phone number.

Stephen and Jane met at a party
and immediately liked each other.

While walking one day, Stephen fell down a flight of stairs and was knocked out for several minutes. Stephen had been having trouble with his balance and speech, but he hadn't said anything to his family.

Over Christmas break in 1962, his family noticed his slurred words and unstable walk. Since Stephen's dad was a doctor, he made an appointment for Stephen to see a specialist. When no one at the hospital would tell him the truth about what was wrong, Stephen knew he must be really sick.

Stephen thought about Jane often and invited her to his twenty-first birthday party. Jane was shy and afraid to talk to the older people at the party. Stephen's mother decided that she didn't like this girl her son had brought home.

Soon after, Stephen and Jane ran into each other again on a train to London. Stephen asked her on a date, but it didn't go as smoothly as he planned. On the date, Stephen tried to impress Jane and spent too much money on dinner. That meant he did not have enough to pay for bus fare to take them home.

In 1963, men were expected to pay for dates, but Stephen reluctantly agreed to let Jane pay for the bus. When Jane tried to pay, however, she found that she had left her purse in the theatre they had visited earlier in the night. Though they were both embarrassed, they enjoyed the adventure and agreed to go on a second date.

Stephen had to go through more tests, but the doctors soon told Stephen that he had something called amyotrophic lateral sclerosis, or ALS for short. ALS attacks the nerves that connect the brain to voluntary muscles, the ones you can control and move to lift weights or write books.

Stephen Hawking would have to watch his voluntary muscles stop working. His involuntary muscles, like his heart, would continue to work just fine. ALS does not kill people by itself, but it does make the body very weak. Many times, people with ALS are so weak that they can't fight off other diseases and illnesses.

Stephen's doctors told him that he probably only had two years to live. Stephen couldn't believe his life would be so short. Before being diagnosed, he had been bored with life and felt like there was nothing worth doing. After his diagnosis, he realized that there was so much he wanted to do before he died. The idea of such a short life depressed him, but he was filled with both the desire to learn and his love for Jane.

Stephen and Jane continued to date each other, but he didn't talk to her about his illness. Jane found out from one of their friends that Stephen had a rare nerve disease. Jane got upset when Stephen refused to talk to her about his ALS. They spent a long time away from each other while Jane traveled to Spain to study Spanish medieval books.

Stephen and Jane loved each other so much that even ALS could not stop them from being together. Stephen asked Jane to marry him in October 1964, before she was even done with college. Jane's father said he was okay with the marriage as long as Jane promised to finish her degree.

Jane and Stephen got married in 1965, but Jane's father
made her promise to finish her degree.

Jane agreed to marry Stephen knowing that his ALS would eventually make him unable to move. Stephen would still be himself, and his brilliant mind would continue to work just as well as it ever had. They were married on July 14, 1965. Stephen was twenty-three and Jane was twenty-one.

Stephen knew that he needed to find a job and make money if he and Jane were going to have children like they wanted. He would need to finish school at Cambridge first. Stephen already had a bachelor's degree from Oxford, but he needed to get a doctoral degree if he was going to be taken seriously as a scientist.

Chapter 4
A Young Family

In order to graduate with a doctoral degree, Stephen needed to write a paper called a thesis. His thesis needed to present a new idea and be supported by math solutions and physics models.

Stephen's thesis claimed that the steady state theory of the universe was not right. He had been thinking about this subject since he was a teenager.

By this time, most scientists agreed that the universe was expanding but disagreed on how and why. Hawking said that, according to physics, for the universe to be steady, it would have to make enough gravity to hold down the edges as the universe got bigger. He claimed that it made more sense to think that the universe started at one point and then moved out in all directions from there.

Stephen could not move well. Writing down the math problems he needed was difficult, so he started thinking about them in non-mathematical ways. Jane typed most of his thesis on a typewriter for him. Stephen finished his doctorate in 1966 at twenty-four years old.

Stephen did not just get a doctorate at Cambridge. The same year, one of his other papers tied for first place for a major award from Cambridge called The Adams Prize. The co-winner was Roger Penrose, who would go on to be another one of the most important scientists and thinkers of the twentieth century. Both papers centered on black holes and the physics surrounding them.

Stephen was offered and accepted a job teaching at Cambridge. He worked in the gravitational physics department and taught his students that they should never be scared to pose a silly question. They just had to follow through to find the answer!

Life suddenly became busy for Jane. She was trying to take care of Stephen and finish her own degree on medieval literature. To do this, she had to read almost all of the books written

Stephen and Jane wanted to start a family,
so they had Robert in 1967.

during the Middle Ages. On top of all of that,
she was going to have a baby!

In the spring of 1967, she gave birth to a
boy. Stephen and Jane named him Robert. The
young Hawking family then made several trips to
the United States for conferences and lectures.
Stephen's will to live and succeed, even with ALS,
inspired people. However, the trips interrupted
Jane's schooling, which bothered her. She still
hadn't finished her degree like she had promised
her father.

By 1968, Stephen was interested in politics
as well as science. The war in Vietnam concerned

him, so he joined in protest marches against the war. He would walk at the front with his crutches.

Hawking became passionately anti-war and supported social programs and education. Stephen believed that the government should help the poor and disabled and provide education for everyone. This marked the beginning of his life as an outspoken political activist.

Stephen was tough and rarely took a day off or complained. He still got sick often and would choke on his food as his throat muscles got weak. He often walked with crutches or used a cane. Jane

Stephen walked with his crutches in protest parades against the Vietnam War.

often became upset that the British government did not do enough to help disabled people. She would write letters to people in the government. Many of the buildings around Cambridge began to build wheelchair ramps and create special parking spaces for people with handicaps. This helped Stephen get around easier.

While Stephen's reputation as a scientist was advancing, his ALS symptoms were also advancing. He managed to walk with the help of canes and crutches all through the 1960s. But in 1969 he became wheelchair bound and lost his ability to walk. He also could not use his hands well, so writing and doing math became almost impossible. Stephen began imagining math problems so that he could see them in his head.

Hawking relied more and more on Jane to type up his papers. This made life even harder for Jane because in 1970, they added another child to the family, Lucy. Jane had to take care of two young kids and Stephen.

Jane had dreams of her own and still wanted to go back to school. She had taken a break

Even though Stephen couldn't walk, he still enjoyed
playing in the yard with his children.

from college to have a family and help Stephen,
but she wanted to finish her degree.

Jane sometimes became frustrated. Her
husband could work on theories about black
holes, but he could not wash the dishes, make
lunches for the kids, or sweep the floors. The
couple tried to be brave and positive, but things
were getting difficult at home.

By 1971, Dr. Hawking was ready to begin
making some really new work. To do this,
Stephen decided to keep working on black holes
because not much was known about them.

Hawking theorized that a small amount of radiation could come out of a black hole. If energy came out of a black hole, this meant that black holes would very slowly get smaller over time. As the black holes got smaller, they would also get hotter. Among scientists, he was the most famous for that theory.

As Dr. Hawking did the math, he found something strange. Hawking found that a black hole would shrink to a size so small that it would blow up. However, it would take so long to happen that no human would be around

Spending time with his family was important to Stephen.

Black holes suck in anything that gets near them,
so they are really dangerous and hard to observe.

to see it. In 1974, Dr. Hawking told another
group of scientists what he had found. Most
of the scientists found the whole idea very hard
to believe.

An important scientific journal, called *Nature*,
published the paper anyway. Pretty soon,
scientists from around the world began to think
that Hawking was right after all, and he began to
acquire the reputation of a genius.

Dr. Hawking continued thinking about black
holes shrinking and came up with an idea that

ended up being named after him. From his math, he found out that black holes would break particles into two parts. This would make radiation and was how black holes got smaller. This meant that black holes would seem to let out energy as they shrank. This became one of his most talked-about ideas, and a lot of other scientists thought he was right. The specific kind of radiation that comes from black holes came to be known as Hawking radiation.

Because of his discoveries, he was elected to the Royal Society in Great Britain. The Royal Society is over three hundred years old and was the first official society for science ever made. It is a group that honors scientific discoveries and achievement. Isaac Newton had once been the president of the group. Being elected to the Royal Society meant that Stephen was earning respect among people in his field as a thinker and scientist.

The Hawking family made a yearlong trip to the United States in 1974 so that Stephen could work with some of the famous scientists at the California Institute for Technology, called Caltech.

He became close friends with two of the smartest scientists at the time, Richard Feynman and Kip Thorne. Hawking, Feynman, and Thorne liked to joke around when they weren't debating physics. Feynman liked to play the bongo drums and dance. Thorne and Stephen made bets about unproven physics theories.

During this trip, Jane suggested that a graduate student live with them to help her

Hawking met Richard Feynman on a visit to the United States and the two became good friends.

take care of Stephen and the children. Stephen reluctantly agreed and Bernard Carr became the first of many to help the Hawking family.

The history of science had always interested Stephen. Galileo Galilei was one of his favorites because Stephen was born on the 300th anniversary of his death. Stephen especially liked reading about how Galileo used a telescope to prove that the planets all revolved around the sun.

The Roman Catholic Church was very powerful and taught that everything orbited the Earth in the early 1600's. Galileo was forced to apologize and deny his own work or be severely punished.

In 1976, Pope Paul VI asked Stephen to travel to the Vatican City in Italy. The pope knew that Stephen was not a Christian, but still wanted to give Stephen an award for his work in science. Hawking went to the Vatican, and while he was there, he got to read the apology letter that Galileo had written several hundred years ago.

Galileo Galilei proved with his telescope
that the Earth revolved around the sun in 1632.

Stephen commented that, since Galileo had been proven right, the current officials of the Roman Catholic Church should pardon Galileo. The pope listened and an apology was issued after Stephen's visit.

In 1977, Cambridge promoted Stephen. Dr. Hawking became Professor Hawking after being given a chair, or a respected spot, in the gravitational physics department. This meant that he would be advising students going after the same degree he had, a doctorate in physics.

He would also have more time to work on his research and theories.

As happy as he was to be a full professor at Cambridge, Hawking was still bothered by how hard it was for him to get around. Even though Cambridge had started putting in ramps and handicap parking, there were still a lot of places that he and his wheelchair couldn't go. Architects and builders just didn't think about how disabled people would get into and out of a building. This made it hard for Dr. Hawking to get around at work.

Even Stephen's parents forgot to think about it sometimes. They bought a house closer to Cambridge to be near their son, but it sat on top of a steep hill. When Stephen would visit, it was very hard for him to get up the hill, even in his motorized wheelchair. Jane would sometimes have to help push the wheelchair. Since they didn't live with him, it was easy for Stephen's parents to underestimate his disability.

Jane continued going to church on Sundays, though Stephen wouldn't go with her. Through church, she joined a group of Christmas carolers and enjoyed singing with them. While caroling, she met Jonathan Hellyer Jones, a fellow caroler. They developed a close friendship and Jones actually moved in with the Hawkings for a while to help take care of the family.

In 1979, the teachers at Cambridge voted to make Stephen Hawking the Lucasian Professor of Mathematics. This is the biggest honor that can be given to a teacher of math and science. Sir Isaac Newton, who discovered gravity and invented calculus, had once been the Lucasian Professor of Mathematics. Stephen was very proud to have been elected.

All Lucasian Professors have signed a specific book, and Professor Hawking was asked to put his name in the book. It was the last signature he would make.

That same year, Jane Hawking gave birth to a third child, Tim. The Hawking family now had three kids, and Stephen could not move much at all to help with them.

Jonathan Hellyer Jones met Jane through church
and they quickly became very good friends.

Stephen's doctors had told him that he might
only live for two years when they found he had
ALS. Stephen had now lived for almost twenty.
Jane worried about what would happen to the
family if Stephen died.

Stephen's youngest son, Tim, grew up with
a dad who could not play or run like most dads
can. Tim could not even understand his dad
when he talked most of the time. Still, they had

fun. Tim would ride on his dad's wheelchair, and they played games like chess together. Stephen and Tim shared a passion for racing and would often go to Formula One races together.

Tim and Stephen enjoyed playing chess together, and it became easier after Stephen got his computerized voice.

Stephen enjoyed traveling, especially when he could go somewhere he hadn't been before. After World War II, Europe was divided in half. The eastern part wasunder the control of the Russians, and the western part under control of the United States and Great Britain. The eastern part formed a huge country called the Soviet Union, which was communist. The government of the Soviet Union and the rest of Europe didn't agree with each other. As a result, people did not travel between the east and west very much. In 1981, though, Stephen got invited to debate physics in Moscow, the capital of the Soviet Union. This was a very rare honor, and Stephen enjoyed touring the country. While there, he also made friends with some of the Russian scientists, and they talked and argued about physics.

Stephen took a trip to Switzerland in order to work with other scientists in 1985. While there, he contracted pneumonia, which made him very weak. As his muscles got weaker, it became difficult for him to swallow. He sometimes choked. How scary it must be to choke when one cannot move or even call for help!

Jane flew to Switzerland to be with Stephen. By the time she got there, Stephen was dying. He had been hooked up to a respirator, a machine that was breathing for him.

Stephen's doctors thought there was nothing they could do. They wanted to turn off the respirator that was keeping Stephen alive. Jane would not let this happen. Stephen was very sick

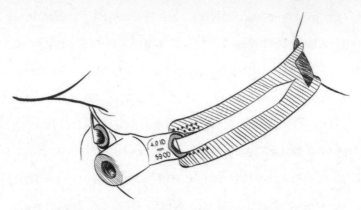

Stephen had to have a tracheotomy to allow him to breathe, which meant he would never use his voice again

and weak, but Jane thought he was strong enough to recover if he had time and better doctors.

Jane took Stephen back to Addenbrooke's Hospital in England so he could get better.

The doctors in England had to find a way to help Stephen breathe without the respirator. They decided to surgically cut a hole in Stephen's throat to let air in. The hole stopped air from getting to his vocal chords, so Stephen could not speak at all. For a while, he communicated by choosing letters on notecards to spell words,. The process was slow and difficult. Stephen quickly became frustrated and searched for an easier alternative.

When he returned home, Stephen could no longer speak, and could barely feed himself or get out of bed on his own. He began needing around-the-clock care. The National Health Service, the public health care available in England, offered to pay for a nursing home for Stephen, but wouldn't cover in-home care.

Jane refused to let Stephen be sent to a nursing home. They had three children under the age of eighteen and she wanted Stephen to be part of their everyday lives at home. Instead, Jane searched for funds to pay for his care from charities and foundations. Eventually, an American foundation took on the cost of caring for Stephen. They provided three shifts of nurses to provide the support he needed.

While Jane was happy that Stephen got to stay home, the extra people in the house put a strain on their relationship. The nurses were always there, so Stephen and Jane were never able to really be alone. It didn't help that Stephen liked to laugh and joke with the nurses. Sometimes, Jane thought he might be flirting with them.

Chapter 5

The Robot Voice

Walter Woltosz, a computer whiz from California, saved Dr. Hawking from a life of silence. After Woltosz's mother-in-law was diagnosed with ALS, she had also lost her ability to speak. He used his knowledge of computers to create a program that would allow her to communicate with the family.

Jane, Lucy, Tim, and Robert all helped Stephen communicate after he lost his voice.

His mother-in-law could still move her fingers, so he developed a system that would scan through words, highlighting them as it went. She would click a button to select a word and create sentences.

When one of Hawking's coworkers asked Woltosz to build Hawking a system, Woltosz was initially reluctant. He asked who the system would be for, but the only answer he got was that it was for a British physicist with ALS. Woltosz immediately asked if it was Stephen Hawking, but Hawking's coworker didn't have Hawking's permission to tell him.

The next day, the coworker called back and told Woltosz that it was, in fact, Stephen Hawking. Woltosz replied that he would be happy to build one for free. He flew to see Stephen so that they could figure out the best way to build the system. They decided that, since Stephen could move his thumb well, he would use a switch similar to Woltosz's mother-in-law.

In the end, Woltosz built a computer system on a desktop computer that allowed Stephen to choose words with the switch and slowly build

Stephen's computer allowed him to communicate by choosing words which are then read by a speech program

sentences. The voice that Woltosz and Stephen chose was very advanced for 1985, but sounded a lot like a robot with an American accent. Stephen didn't care about the voice, though. He was just happy to be able to talk to his family again.

The only problem with this setup was that the computer was stationary, it wasn't attached to his chair. If Stephen wanted to talk, he had to sit next to the computer. This really limited what he was able to do and frustrated him.

Stephen had grown especially close to one of his nurses, Elaine Mason, who told him that her husband may be able to help. He was a computer engineer who built and adapted computers all the time.

David Mason visited Stephen and they talked about what needed to change. David then created a system to attach the Apple II computer, which was running his speech program, to his chair.

Stephen later attended a conference in 1997 where Intel cofounder Gordon Moore noticed that Hawking was still using his original system. It was twelve years old, terribly outdated, and very slow.

Moore bravely walked up to Hawking and offered to build him a "real computer." From then on, Intel and Stephen have worked together to develop computers and programs. Hawking's computer still works in much the same way, but is faster and more efficient.

Moore offered to replace the robotic voice Hawking had been using since 1985, and Hawking agreed to listen to new voices. In the end, though, he didn't like them. He thought of the robotic voice as his own voice and wanted to keep it.

Hawking's desk was cluttered,
but his research was always clear and organized.

When his synthesizer, the machine creating the voice, started not working well, Hawking searched for a new one with his voice. He ended up finding out that there were only three left in the world. Hawking bought all of them.

Hawking controlled his computer by the thumb switch until 2005. Hawking had slowly lost control of the thumb he was using to operate the switch and couldn't move it anymore. One of his graduate students developed a new switch for his cheek, so that he could still use the computer system.

Stephen controlled the computer by moving the small muscles near his eyes. This was still how he controlled his computer until his death.

Chapter 6
A Brief History of Time

Stephen almost died. This realization made him want to share what he knew with the world.

Dr. Hawking decided to write a book that would help people to make sense of the biggest ideas in science. He wanted to share his understanding of mathematics, black holes, and the universe with the world.

Stephen began his important writing project at the same time that his marriage to Jane looked like it would end. He and Jane had grown apart from one another during the last few years. Now Stephen was thinking about writing a new book, which would take more time away from them.

Hawking wanted to write a book about black holes, time, and the universe, but many other scientists had already done that. These other books were full of complicated math problems and intricate physics models. Only other scientists could understand them well, and sometimes even they couldn't.

Hawking believed that everyone should be able to understand science, so he wrote his book so that non-scientists could read and understand it. Hawking wanted this new book to be read by as many people as possible. He wanted it to be the kind of book that people bought in airports. Usually, people in airports are looking to buy books that are short and fun to read, not books filled with complicated scientific theory. What Hawking wanted to do seemed impossible.

Stephen's ALS meant that he would have to write at the pace allowed by his computer, only fifteen words per minute. Hawking wrote slowly, but the book's pages began to pile up. He wrote

Stephen wanted *A Brief History of Time* to be something people read at airports.

Stephen patiently worked with his editor through several drafts before his book finally got published.

without distractions and connected basic math and physics to his work on black holes.

In 1984, he sent a rough draft of his book to different publishers who might want to buy it. Several publishers were interested, but Hawking wanted to work with one specifically. Bantam Press was known for printing the kinds of books that make it into airport book shops.

Stephen's editor at Bantam made Hawking rewrite his book so that it would be clearer to readers who did not understand complicated math. Having written the whole book without the use of his hands, Stephen Hawking then had to rewrite the entire thing in the same way.

When it was finished, the book was titled *A Brief History of Time: From the Big Bang to Black Holes.* Several early copies were printed and sent to other scientists.

Dr. Hawking wrote the book with great care for the facts, but the subject was hard to simplify. Hawking made some mistakes and oversimplified so much that some of it was wrong. When another scientist read the book, they found the errors and told Stephen about them. When the mistakes were fixed, select bookstores started to sell the book in 1988.

One of the things that Hawking explained was that space and time were not really two different things, but rather a mesh of both. You couldn't have space without time. Gravity was what happened to the fabric of space-time around something heavy.

Hawking explained that space-time was like a sheet stretched tightly, and the planets are

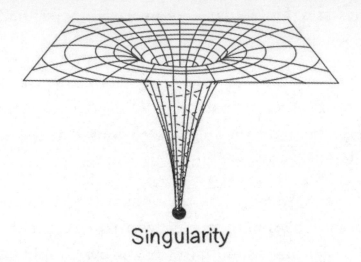

Singularity

Black holes are so heavy that they stretch the fabric of space-time and create a singularity.

like heavy bowling balls in the sheet. Gravity is the force that pulls other objects towards that center while in space.

The original cover for *A Brief History of Time* was a picture of Hawking in his wheelchair. The picture helped make Stephen famous because he was instantly recognizable. The wheelchair was for Hawking what the white hair and mustache were for Einstein.

A Brief History of Time became one of the most influential science books of the twentieth century.

The mix of clear writing and an interesting topic quickly turned *A Brief History of Time* into a best-seller. It was soon sold at all bookshops, even those in the airports. To date, more than ten million copies of the book have been sold in over forty languages.

Stephen's first book was a best-seller and featured a picture of him in his wheelchair on the front cover.

Sadly, as Stephen was writing the book, his father began to suffer from bad health. Frank Hawking died in 1986, just before Stephen published the book. Stephen didn't talk much about his family or personal life, but he wrote about the impact that his father's interest in science had on him. His death hit Stephen hard.

Chapter 7
Stephen and Elaine

During the years it took Hawking to write his book, his relationship with Jane had been getting difficult. She didn't like the nurses intruding on their family all the time, but there wasn't much she could do about it. Stephen needed the medical help that they provided. Jane felt like she was being pushed out of Stephen's life.

Stephen was focusing on his book, not their relationship, and the nurses didn't pay attention to Jane as she wasn't their patient. She was lonely and turned to one of her friends for comfort. Jonathan Hellyer Jones had been a good friend to Jane since they met while caroling fifteen years earlier. Jane began bringing Jonathan over more often to help with the children and their activities.

Stephen, in the meantime, spent more and more time by himself or with his nurses, which gave him a chance to become good friends with Elaine Mason. She had been the nurse to offer her husband's help on Stephen's computer

Shortly after Jane and Stephen divorced,
Stephen married his nurse Elaine Mason.

problems. Since then, though, she and David had
divorced. Elaine and Stephen enjoyed spending
time together and laughed at the same jokes.

In 1990, Hawking and Jane separated.
Stephen moved in with Elaine, who helped him
as he flew back and forth across Europe and the
United States to speak. As *A Brief History of Time*
gained popularity, Stephen was asked to attend
more scientific meetings and promote his ideas
and book.

In 1995, Jane and Stephen officially divorced,
and Hawking married Elaine. Not long after that,
Jane married Jonathan Hellyer Jones. He had

once lived in the Hawking house and helped the family deal with Stephen's ALS. Jane and Jones had been friends for a very long time, but had never been romantic out of respect for Stephen.

Bill Clinton was the President of the United States in 1998. President Clinton asked Stephen to be a part of a White House event called the *Millennium Evening Series*. This series had eight talks and performances given by some of the smartest and most talented people in the world.

Hawking spoke about the problems that human greed combined with the power of science

Hawking was invited to speak at the Millennium Evening Series and talked about what he thought we might see in the 2000s.

could pose for everyone. Dr. Hawking ended his talk by saying that he hoped none of the really bad things, like a nuclear war or tests on human DNA, would really happen. He did not think they would, but people should be careful.

The idea of nuclear war is very scary. No one knows what the world would look like afterwards if it ever happened.

The same year, other scientists found mathematical evidence that showed that the universe not only got bigger, but that humans are living inside of a huge explosion! The edges of the universe seemed to be expanding away from one another.

Hawking began to apply his work on black holes to the theory that the universe was exploding. He found that the math of black holes worked well with the math of the exploding universe.

By 1999, the Hawking children had all grown up. Jane and Stephen had been broken up for

MUSIC TO MOVE
THE STARS

JANE HAWKING
A Life With Stephen

Jane's book *Music to Move the Stars* told the story of Stephen and Jane's marriage and life together from Jane's point of view.

nine years and divorced for four years. Jane had gotten married again and earned her PhD. She wrote a book about her life and marriage to Stephen called *Music to Move the Stars*. This book drew a lot of attention to Stephen's private life. The public was very interested in Stephen Hawking, the person, as well as Dr. Hawking, the scientist.

Also in 1999, Stephen said that his wife saved his life. Elaine was a trained nurse and saw that part of the machine that helped Stephen to swallow hurt his throat. An operation fixed the problem just in time. The machine would have caused blood to drip into Stephen's lungs and drown him.

The year 2000 was an election year in the United States and the Democratic candidate, Al Gore, was running against the Republican candidate, George W. Bush. Although Dr. Hawking is British, he supported Al Gore by making a video statement that played during Mr. Gore's party nomination.

George W. Bush won the election, and not long after, the United States suffered from the 9/11 terrorist attacks in New York City and Washington, DC. When President Bush ordered the US military to attack Iraq in 2003, Dr. Hawking strongly opposed the invasion. He even called the attack on Iraq a criminal act.

Chapter 8
Author and Activist

The evidence coming in from the universe didn't make sense. It seemed impossible to think that a single "theory of everything" could ever explain it all. How could humans describe a universe that seemed to blow up like a balloon? What, exactly, does the universe expand into? Did it have a beginning or has it always just been there? Hawking was determined to answer those questions.

To try to come up with some answers and build on the popularity of his *A Brief History of Time*, Hawking wrote and co-wrote several other books at the beginning of the twenty-first century. *Black Holes and Baby Universes* was a collection of essays about physics and math. Another book, *A Briefer History of Time*, was a new edited version of his first classic that included pictures to help explain the ideas. In 2001, Stephen wrote *The Universe in a Nutshell,* which explained what happened at the edges of black holes.

Stephen published his second book
in part to help pay for his children to go to college.

The beginning of the twenty-first century was good for Stephen Hawking as an author, but also as an advocate. Hawking argued publicly for equal rights for disabled people. For a long time, he had been saying that schools and other public places should make it easier for people in wheelchairs to get in and out. Now that he was famous, more people paid attention to what he had to say.

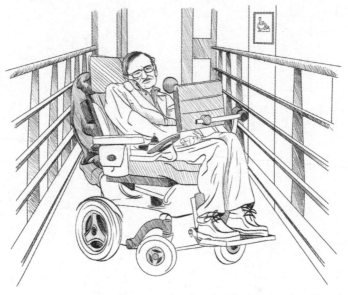

It took a couple years, but Cambridge finally listened to Stephen and installed wheelchair ramps on all of their buildings.

In 2001, the British Broadcasting Corporation (BBC) made a show about Dr. Hawking that showed him in a fast new wheelchair. In the show, Hawking argued that technology for disabled people should be made better. His belief was that the government of the United Kingdom should make laws that required equal access to buildings for people in wheelchairs.

Stephen also thought that it was important to encourage disabled people, whether they be mentally or physically disabled. When he traveled somewhere to speak, he would often arrange to meet with local children, especially those in wheelchairs. He wanted them to know that their dreams were possible, whether they were in a wheelchair or not. He didn't think anyone should give up because of a disability, no matter what. If Stephen had given up when they told him he only had two years to live, he would never have written his books or made his discoveries!

In 2002, Hawking turned sixty. At one time, it would have been easy to believe that he would never have turned thirty. Hundreds of Hawking's friends, family, and colleagues got together for his birthday party.

Sadly, Dr. Hawking accidentally ran his wheelchair into a wall shortly before the party. He broke his leg in the crash, so he could not be at his own party.

Stephen wasn't able to attend his party,
but another conference was held later that he did attend.

Everyone had the party on his birthday without him and Stephen would have loved it. The birthday party was perfect because it was both a party and a scientific conference! People read papers about math and science and told jokes.

After Stephen recovered, his wife Elaine surprised him with a trip in a hot air balloon as a late birthday present. Flying in a hot air balloon had been a lifelong dream of Stephen's, but he thought he'd never be able to because of his wheelchair. Elaine modified the basket of one of the company's balloons to allow wheelchair-bound people like Stephen to fly. The balloon company continued to use the basket after Stephen's flight to allow others to experience going up in a hot air balloon.

Chapter 9
Robert, Lucy, and Tim

Stephen's daughter, Lucy, was close with her dad and worried about him because he seemed to get hurt often. She sometimes thought that Stephen's wife, Elaine, was hurting Stephen. All three of Stephen's children worried that Elaine was not good for him.

In 2003, Lucy called the police. The police asked Stephen's nurses how he was getting hurt. The nurses also thought that Elaine was hurting Stephen. She was accused of breaking one of the bones in his arm, cutting him on the cheek, and leaving him out in the hot sun for so long that he got heat stroke and a sunburn.

Stephen denied all of the accusations, so there was no way to know if any of it was true or not. However, he did end his marriage with Elaine in 2006.

Stephen was still close with his children. Stephen's oldest son, Robert, works for

Microsoft. Robert lived in Canada for a while but then moved to the United States, where Microsoft is located. Robert was always close with his dad and helped him do things as his ALS got worse. Robert has a son and daughter of his own.

Stephen and Lucy wrote a series of young adult books together and made presentations on the importance of science education.

Lucy didn't follow in her father's scientific footsteps. She liked words more than numbers and attended Oxford to study French and Russian. She worked hard and became a well-known news writer in the UK.

Now, Lucy writes novels, and, in 2007, she started writing books for young adults with her dad. The first book was called *George's Secret Key to the Universe*. The series that Lucy and Stephen wrote together encouraged kids to explore science.

Lucy has a son with autism who was born in 1997, and she tries to help parents of other children with autism. Like her dad, Lucy does not let any disabilities hold her or her family back.

Stephen's youngest son, Tim, studied foreign languages in college and works for the LEGO Corporation in the United Kingdom. After a childhood in the limelight with his father, Tim tries to stay out of the public eye as an adult. In an interview with BBC, though, he told the interviewer about how much fun he and his father had watching racing as he was growing up.

Stephen's children, Lucy (left), Robert (middle), and Tim (right), visited him as often as they could and enjoy getting together as a family

Chapter 10
Traveling the World, Space, and Cosmos

Stephen Hawking said that he thought Isaac Newton
was the greatest scientist in history.

Isaac Newton once said that if he saw further into the mysteries of science, it was because he "stood on the shoulders of giants." This was taken to mean that his own discoveries were only possible because he had been able to build off of the work of thinkers before him.

Hawking wrote a collection of essays published with classic works of science titled *On the Shoulders of Giants*. It was published shortly after his sixtieth birthday. Through the title, Hawking showed respect to the scientists and thinkers that came before him.

Hawking knew that he would never have been able to achieve what he had without the help of the mathematicians, physicists, and thinkers before him. He used the calculus that Isaac Newton invented to do the complicated math he needed. He used Albert Einstein's theory of relativity to figure out how light would bend around a black hole. He used work from dozens of people before him to build his own theories. He wanted to thank them for their help, so he wrote *On the Shoulders of Giants*.

After working on theories about space for most of his life, Dr. Hawking decided to actually go out into space in the spring of 2007. He wanted to feel what it would be like to have no weight.

He found a business that sent people on special plane rides designed to create brief periods of zero gravity. Hawking enjoyed the weightlessness that freed him from his wheelchair for the first time in forty years. He had so much fun that he went up eight times!

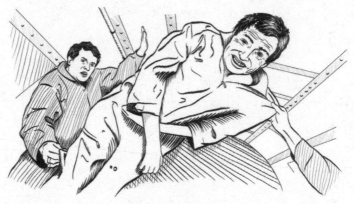

Hawking loved being in zero gravity and said he would love to go again.

Hawking was single, not writing a book or teaching classes, and had no children at home, so he decided to travel the world in 2008. He went to Chile in South America to meet with one of Chile's most famous scientists, Stephen's friend Claudio Bunster.

He flew to South Africa to meet the great South African civil-rights leader and president,

Nelson Mandela. The two men worked together to build new programs to encourage South African scientists.

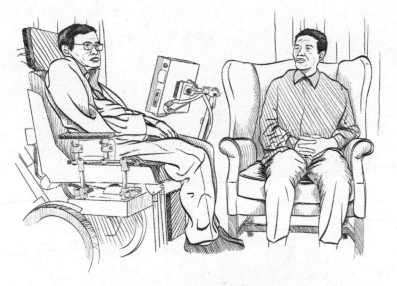

Hawking and Mandela worked together
to create opportunities for scientists in South Africa.

Hawking went to Spain, where he answered questions from reporters and people who were interested in science. While there, he received the first Fonseca Prize for putting cosmology in the hands and minds of average people.

Through it all, Stephen was still thinking about black holes and the universe. He became friends with Caltech scientist and author Leonard

Mlodinow during a visit to the United States. Dr. Hawking continued to claim that a theory of everything would be found one day. His search for the answer to this puzzle led him to write a book called *The Grand Design* with Dr. Mlodinow.

Leonard Mlodinow and Stephen worked together to create the book *The Grand Design* tackling difficult physics topics.

In *The Grand Design*, published in 2010, Hawking and Mlodinow wrote about big ideas and problems. The big question for a lot of scientists was this: what happens when something falls into a black hole?

Hawking bases many of this theories
off of the theories of Albert Einstein.

Hawking had at first believed that anything that fell into a black hole would be lost. A couple of Russian physicists proved his math wrong. He then theorized that some things could be returned, but they would be destroyed.

He compared what came back out of a black hole to an encyclopedia that had been burned. The ashes would be there, but no one would be able to read the words.

In *The Grand Design*, Hawking made his last attempt to come up with a theory of everything. He connected Einstein's theory of relativity with quantum mechanics, a special branch of physics. While he doesn't offer up a theory of everything, he does talk about its possible existence and predicts how that will happen.

The Grand Design was Stephen's second book to become a *New York Times* bestseller.

In *The Grand Design,* Stephen Hawking admitted that he did not see a place for a god in the universe. He hadn't believed in a god for a long time, but had never said so in a book before. It upset a lot of people who believed.

In 2011, Hawking told an interviewer that he did not believe that people have souls. He said that when the brain dies, that's the end of life. Many people found this terrifying because life is so short, but Hawking saw it an entirely different way. He said, "We have this one life to appreciate the grand design of the universe, and for that I am extremely grateful."

Chapter 11
Pop Culture Icon

Stephen played a hologram of himself on an episode of
Star Trek: the Next Generation.

Dr. Hawking wrote a lot of books, but he was also famous for starring in television shows and movies, and there were many movies made about him.

His book *A Brief History of Time*, had been turned into a documentary in 1991, but Stephen didn't appear in the film. At the showing, Stephen was introduced to Leonard Nimoy, who played Spock on the original *Star Trek* show. When Nimoy found out that Stephen was a *Star Trek* fan, he talked to the show's producer and got Stephen a spot on the show in 1993. Stephen was ecstatic and even helped write some of the dialogue.

Stephen was excited to show the audiences that science could be interesting.

Next, he appeared on *The Simpsons* as a cartoon in 1999. At one point, Dr. Hawking and Homer Simpson talked about the idea that the universe might be shaped like Homer's favorite food, a donut. Stephen told an interviewer that he was excited to show the audience that "science can also have street cred."

He continued appearing on many television shows, including three more times on *The Simpsons*, once on *Futurama*, and once on *The Big Bang Theory*, among other shows.

Into the Universe revealed the science behind topics usually thought of as science fiction, like time travel and aliens.

In 2010, he starred on *Into the Universe with Stephen Hawking*, a television documentary series. Dr. Hawking wrote the Discovery Channel shows, which covered many things. He said humans on Earth might be able to talk with aliens on other planets soon. He talked about time travel, but he and many other scientists believe that it is silly and will never happen.

On one of the episodes of *Into the Universe*, Stephen actually threw a party for time travelers. He didn't send the invitations until the next day, so that he could be sure anyone attending was an actual time traveler. Unfortunately, no one showed up. Hawking claims that this is

Stephen threw a huge party for time travelers and waited for guests to arrive, but no one showed up!

experimental evidence proving that time travel does not, and will not, exist.

In 2014, The Public Broadcasting Service (PBS) put out a show called *Hawking*. The show came out not long after Dr. Hawking had said that black holes might not actually be way out in the sky! He had been thinking about black holes in a new way, and it got other scientists talking.

In a paper he wrote in 1970, Hawking had said that black holes would slowly evaporate. This went against the basic laws of physics, and other scientists constantly argued with the theory.

Then Stephen came up with a way that his theory wouldn't break the rules. Black holes are supposed to pull everything in with their gravity and not let it go again. But what if, instead, they only held on to it for a really long time?

This idea got the science world talking right as *Hawking* came out. *Hawking* was not just about science. It showed Dr. Hawking and how he lived with ALS, and the audience got to see some of Hawking's life outside of math and science.

The most recent show that Stephen hosted came out through PBS in the spring of 2016. It was called *Genius*. Instead of telling people about black holes and science, Stephen hosted the show and challenged people to think the same way that geniuses from the past had to think to answer big questions. The show was popular, and a new generation of people had the chance to see Dr. Hawking on TV.

Benedict Cumberbatch was the first actor to portray Hawking on the big screen. Stephen had always played himself before.

In movies about his life, Stephen Hawking has been played by two of the most popular actors of the twenty-first century. Benedict Cumberbatch starred in a 2004 BBC movie also titled *Hawking*.

Cumberbatch played the part of a young Stephen who just found out about his ALS and met Jane. Most people already thought that Stephen Hawking was a genius, but after the movie came out, they could see just how tough it had been to live with ALS.

In 2014, a big Hollywood movie titled *The Theory of Everything* was made about Stephen Hawking's life with Jane. The star of the movie was the British actor Eddie Redmayne. The movie begins with Stephen as a Cambridge student looking for an idea to write about for his doctorate. It focused more on his family and personal life and less on his science.

Redmayne showed the way in which ALS took away Stephen's ability to move. He even managed to grin like Hawking does! On the screen, Stephen and Jane fell in love, married, and started a family. Then the problems that

Eddie Redmayne was very nervous to meet Stephen, but Stephen joked around with him to make him more comfortable.

became a big part of their lives together began to pull them away from one another.

In the movies, many basic facts about Hawking's life were changed slightly in order to make his story easier to understand. Still, the high points of Hawking's life were there. Eddie Redmayne did such a good job of showing what ALS does to a person that he won an Oscar for it. Jane liked the movie quite a lot and thought that Felicity Jones, who played Jane, should have won an Oscar award for her performance too.

Felicity Jones played Jane in *The Theory of Everything* so well that Jane said, "My goodness, that's me!"

Chapter 12
Awards and Legacy

Hawking continued to influence the way people think about certain things. In 2013, Stephen began to speak out more about politics. He believed that all people should have government-paid health care and that stem cells should be used in scientific research.

Stephen lived in the United Kingdom, which was composed of England, Wales, Scotland, and Northern Ireland. In 2014, the people of Scotland held a vote to determine whether they wanted to stay in the United Kingdom or not. Stephen spoke out supporting staying because the unification of countries helps ideas to spread. The Scottish people voted not to leave.

In 2016, Hawking spoke out against the British exit from the European Union, called Brexit for BRitish EXIT, for the same reasons. The British people voted to leave the Union. Stephen worried that international cooperation on science projects would be more difficult.

Hawking has been given just about every major award that a scientist can be given. The fact that Hawking had not won the Nobel Prize for physics did not upset him too much. The Nobel Prize is rarely given to theorists who work in math and physics. Instead, it is given mostly to researchers who find hard evidence and do experiments. However, in 2016, a scientist in Israel created a tiny black hole of sound to test Hawking radiation. His tests seemed to prove Stephen's theory correct, but other scientists still need to review the experiment to make sure.

Hawking was very proud and honored
to receive the Copley Medal.

Instead of the Nobel Prize, Hawking won something even better in 2006. The Copley Medal is the oldest science award. It was given to people like Charles Darwin, Albert Einstein, and Benjamin Franklin. Stephen was honored to be nominated, let alone win the prize. To recognize Stephen's contributions in cosmology and space research, an astronaut even took the medal on a trip to the International Space Station before it was given to Stephen.

In 2009, President Barack Obama awarded Hawking with the Presidential Medal of Freedom. This is the biggest award that the United States can give to someone not in the military. Hawking isn't even an American!

An award given out by the Starmus Festival for Science and Arts is called the Stephen Hawking Medal for Science Communication. The medal rewards people who work to make science understandable and available to the public in the way that Stephen did with *A Brief History of Time*. Hawking had a vision for a world where science plays a positive role in society, and

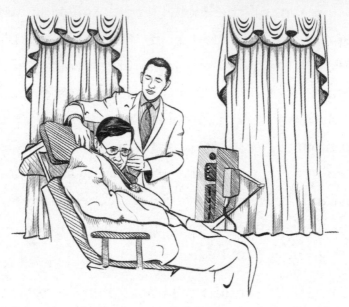

President Barack Obama awarded Stephen with the Presidential
Medal of Freedom at the White House in 2009.

the award named after him helps to recognize
others who expand that vision.

Starting in 2010, Stephen Hawking talked a
lot about aliens. He thought that aliens could be
really scary and we should not look too hard to
find them. He worried that the aliens we found
might not be friendly or might have diseases we
were not prepared for.

An alien visit is fun to talk about but is not very
likely. Stephen spoke out much more publicly

about the dangers that global warming and nuclear weapons pose to humanity. He warned that people need to be careful with the planet or start looking for a new one. He told a British publication that he thinks humans only have 100 more years on Earth before it gets destroyed.

As he aged, Stephen Hawking came to enjoy time by himself. He had no wife. He did not belong to a church. He lived by himself and was attended by nurses. He remained the world's best-known scientist and was probably one of the most famous people in the world. His work helped to explain the mysteries of the universe and bring the wonder of science to huge numbers of people. He was an important advocate for giving rights to the disabled. He floated in space, helped to raise a family, and built a large (and expanding) universe of friends.

Though he was best known for his physics, Stephen said that, in his life, he was most proud of his children. He spent a lot of time with his kids and grandkids. He remained friends with Jane and her husband Jonathan. Stephen worked at Cambridge with a small number of students who are interested in black holes and physics until 2009.

On March 14, 2016, Stephen Hawking died at the age of seventy-six years old. At one time, few people thought that Dr. Hawking would ever reach the age of thirty. His children Tim, Robert, and Lucy co-wrote a moving statement about their father. They praised both his intelligence and his wit and then stated that their father had once said, "It would not be much of a universe if it wasn't home to the people you love." The universe is certainly a richer place for having had Stephen Hawking in it.

Select Quotes from Stephen Hawking

My disability has not been a serious handicap in my scientific work. In fact, in some ways I guess it has been an asset: I haven't had to lecture or teach undergraduates, and I haven't had to sit on tedious and time-consuming committees. So I have been able to devote myself completely to research.

To my colleagues, I'm just another physicist, but to the wider public, I became possibly the best-known scientist in the world. This is partly because scientists, apart from Einstein, are not widely known rock stars, and partly because I fit the stereotype of a disabled genius. I can't disguise myself with a wig and dark glasses—the wheelchair gives me away.

—*My Brief History: A Memoir*

The World has changed far more in the past 100 years than in any other century in history. The reason is not political or economic, but technological—technologies that flowed directly from advances in basic science.

—"A Brief History of Relativity," *Time Magazine*

I have no idea. People who boast about their IQ are losers.

—after being asked about his IQ in an interview with Deborah Solomon

Galileo, perhaps more than any other single person, was responsible for the birth of modern science.

—*A Brief History of Time*

If you are disabled, it is probably not your fault, but it is no good blaming the world or expecting it to take pity on you. One has to have a positive attitude and must make the bset of the situation tha one finds oneself in; if one is physically disabled, one cannot afford to be psychologically disabled as well. In my opinion, one should concentrate on activities in which one's physical disability will not present a serious handicap. I am afraid that the Olympic Games for the disabled do not appeal to me, but it is easy for me to say that because I never liked athletics anyway. On the other hand, science is a very good area for disabled people because it goes on mainly in the mind.

—"Handicapped People and Science," *Science Digest*

Stephen Hawking Timeline

1942 January 8   Born in Oxford, England

1958 March 16   Built a computer from recycled clock, phone, and switchboard parts

1959 October   Attended University College, Oxford for Physics

1960   Joined rowing team

1962 July 12   Graduated Oxford with a degree in Natural Science; enrolled at Cambridge University for Cosmology

1963 May 12   Diagnosed with ALS

1965 July 15   Married Jane Wilde

1966 March   Received Ph.D. in Applied Mathematics and Theoretical Physics

1967 May   Son Robert Hawking born

1968 March   Protested Vietnam War with Labour Party

1970 November 2   Daughter Lucy Hawking born

1974 October 28   Discovered that black holes emit radiation

1974   Move-in graduate students began helping with his care

1979 May 24   Became Lucasian Professor of Mathematics

1979 April 15   Son Timothy Hawking born

1985   Contracted pneumonia resulting in tracheostomy

1986   Computer program for voice built

1988 December 23   *A Brief History of Time* published

World Timeline

1939 June 13   Lou Gehrig diagnosed with ALS, which will later become known as Lou Gehrig's disease

1942 January 8   300th anniversary of Galileo's death

1953 June 2   Queen Elizabeth II coronated as queen of England

1955 November 1   Vietnam War began

1957 October 4   Sputnik I became the first satellite in space

1958 July 29   NASA created by the US Congress

1959 May 28   Two monkeys, Miss Able and Miss Baker, became the first living beings to return to Earth after space flight

1961 April 12   Yuri Gagarin became the first human in space

1962 February 4   A Grand Conjunction occurred, meaning all of the visible planets, moon, and sun all line up during an eclipse

1964   The Higgs Boson, or the God particle, is theorized. Hawking will later write a book on the subject

1965   Roger Penrose published a paper on black holes, spurring Hawking's own paper

1968 July 18   Computer chip company Intel is founded

1969 July 20   Neil Armstrong became first man to walk on the moon

1985 January   First cell phones calls in the United Kingdom are made

Stephen Hawking Timeline (cont.)

1995   Divorced Jane Wilde; Married Elaine Mason

1997   Intel created a computer and program for Hawking to communicate

1999 August 13   Jane published *Music to Move the Stars* about being married to Hawking

2006 November 30   Awarded Copley Medal

2006   Divorced Elaine Mason

2007 April 26   Participated in 0G flight

2009 July 30   Awarded the Presidential Medal of Freedom

2009 June 28   Hosted time-traveler party, sent out invitations afterwards

2013 September 10   *My Brief History* autobiography released

World Timeline (cont.)

1986   Halley's comet passed the Earth for the first time in 76 years

1990 April 24   Hubble Space Telescope launched

1995 February   Scientists began looking for alien communications at Parkes Observatory

1997 August 31   Princess Diana was killed in a car wreck, the United Kingdom mourned

1999 January 1   The Euro is launched as an international currency

2006 August   The International Astronomical Union announced that Pluto is not a planet but rather a dwarf planet

2013 January 2   Caltech reported that the Milky Way Galaxy contains at least one planet per star

2017 April   Scientists used images from eight observatories to construct the first image of a black hole

Glossary

Alumni   A person who has attended or has graduated from a particular school, college, or university

Amyotrophic Lateral Sclerosis (ALS)   A disease that slowly weakens the connections between nerves so that sufferers loses the ability to control their muscles

Astronomy   The science of the size, movement, and makeup of planets, stars, and other objects in space

Black Hole   A place of very dense gravity that results from a star collapsing

Calculus   A branch of math that deals with the way the numbers of moving things change

Caravan   A covered vehicle that usually includes a bed

Cosmology   The branch of astronomy that deals with the beginning, structure, and relations of things in the universe

Coxswain   A sailor in charge of the ship's direction and crew

Doctorate   Also called a PhD, An advanced degree earned after the first college degree that shows expertise in a subject

Epidemiologist   A person who specializes in the branch of medicine that deals with disease

Formula One Racing   An international form of auto racing with single-seat, open-wheel, open-cockpit cars

Galileo Galilei   An Italian astronomer and physicist that argued that the Earth revolved around the sun when many people believed the opposite

Genius   A very gifted person

Gravitational Physics   The science that explains gravity and how items relate to each other

Hawking Radiation   The radiation that leaves black holes

Heatstroke   After being too warm for too long, the body stops sweating and overheats

Medieval Literature   Books or writings from the Middle Ages (500 AD to 1500 AD)

Millenium   A period of 1000 years, used often to refer to the year 2000

Newton   An English mathmetician and physicist who is famous for his theory of gravity and developing calculus

Opera   A play in which the text is sung with an orchestra

Oversimplify   To simplify something so much that the result is confusing or wrong

PhD   see Doctorate

Pneumonia   A lung disease marked by inflammation, congestion, fever, and difficulty breathing

Radiation   Energy let go from an object in waves or particles

Respirator   A device used to aid in breathing or breathe for someone

Singularity   Something that acts like nothing else, or something that is single. Black holes are called singularities because they are the only thing in the universe that act like they do, and because they have so much gravity they condense everything down to a single point

Stem Cells   Very young cells that can be used to heal major illnesses and injuries

Thesis   A long essay based on original research or science required to earn a doctorate

Unification   The state of being brought together to form a whole

Bibliography

Ferguson, Kitty. *Stephen Hawking: An Unfettered Mind*. New York: Palgrave MacMillan, 2012.

Hawking, Jane. *Music to Move the Stars: A Life with Stephen*. London: Pan Books, 1999.

Hawking, Stephen. *A Brief History of Time: From the Big Bang to Black Holes*. New York: Bantam, 1988.

Hawking, Stephen William. *The Universe in a Nutshell*. New York: Bantam, 2001.

Hawking, Stephen. *On the Shoulders of Giants: The Great Works of Physics and Astronomy*. Philadelphia: Running Press Book Publishers, 2002.

Hawking, Stephen, and Leonard Mlodinow. *The Grand Design*. New York: Bantam Books, 2010.

Hawking, Stephen. *My Brief History*. New York: Random House, 2013.

Author Biography

Chris Edwards, Ed. D., has had his scholarship and teaching methodology published in journals produced by both the National Council for History Education and the National Council for Social Studies. He is a frequent contributor on topics of law, logic, and theoretical physics to the science and philosophy journals *Skeptic* and *Free Inquiry*. He proudly teaches world history and Advanced Placement world history at a public high school in Indiana.

Index

Index (cont.)

Index (cont.)

Index (cont.)

Index (cont.)

Index (cont.)

Index (cont.)

Index (cont.)

Index (cont.)